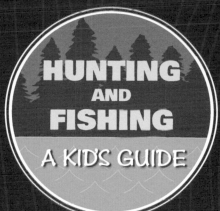

HUNTING
AND
FISHING
A KID'S GUIDE

We're Going

ICE
FISHING

Nia Kennedy

PowerKiDS
press.

New York

Published in 2017 by The Rosen Publishing Group, Inc.
29 East 21st Street, New York, NY 10010

First Edition

Editor: Melissa Raé Shofner
Book Design: Tanya Dellaccio

Photo Credits: Cover Maksimilian/Shutterstock.com; back cover, pp. 1, 3, 4, 6, 8–10, 12, 14, 16–18, 20, 22–24, 26, 28, 30–32 ArtBitz/Shutterstock.com; all pages except p. 2 sittipong/Shutterstock.com; p. 5 James Smedley/Design Pics/ Getty Images; p. 7 Douglas Allen/Getty Images; p. 9 (top) GROGL/Shutterstock.com; p. 9 (bottom) Nancy Bauer/Shutterstock.com; p. 11 Brenda Carson/Shutterstock.com; p. 13 Tyler Olson/Shutterstock.com; pp. 15, 29 Stephen Mcsweeny/Shutterstock.com; p. 17 (top) Tuzemka/Shutterstock.com; p. 17 (bottom) dcwcreations/Shutterstock.com; p. 18 Lost Mountain Studio/Shutterstock.com; p. 19 Doug Allan/Getty Images; p. 21 DoublePHOTO studio/Shutterstock.com; p. 23 (top) Eriks Z/Shutterstock.com; p. 23 (bottom) Gurov Vladimir/Shutterstock.com; p. 25 Verena Matthew/Shutterstock.com; p. 27 Kletr/Shutterstock.com; p. 30 James Smedley/Getty Images.

Library of Congress Cataloging-in-Publication Data

Names: Kennedy, Nia, author.
Title: We're going ice fishing / Nia Kennedy.
Description: New York : PowerKids Press, 2017. | Series: Hunting and fishing
 : a kid's guide | Includes index.
Identifiers: LCCN 2016042064| ISBN 9781499427486 (pbk. book) | ISBN
 9781508152828 (6 pack) | ISBN 9781499428704 (library bound book)
Subjects: LCSH: Ice fishing–Juvenile literature.
Classification: LCC SH455.45 .K46 2017 | DDC 799.12/2–dc23
LC record available at https://lccn.loc.gov/2016042064

Manufactured in the United States of America

CPSIA Compliance Information: Batch Batch #BW17PK: For Further Information contact Rosen Publishing, New York, New York at 1-800-237-9932

CONTENTS

A NOTE TO READERS
Always talk with a parent or teacher before proceeding with any of the activities found in this book.
Some activities require adult supervision.

A NOTE TO PARENTS AND TEACHERS
This book was written to be informative and entertaining. Some of the activities in this book
require adult supervision. Please talk with your child or student before allowing them to proceed
with any hunting activities. The author and publisher specifically disclaim any liability for injury or
damages that may result from use of information in this book.

FISHING ON ICE

If you enjoy outdoor activities during the winter, ice fishing might be for you. People can take part in this activity only in places where it gets so cold that lakes and other bodies of water become covered in thick ice.

In many countries, people once fished to find food to eat during the winter. Today, ice fishing is done mostly for fun. Ice fishing is popular in parts of Canada and the American Midwest where the winters tend to be very cold.

HUNTING HINT

The Canadian Ice Fishing Championship is held each year on Lake Simcoe in Ontario, Canada. This is a CPR—catch, photograph, **release**—tournament.

In Wisconsin, fish caught while ice fishing make up about one-quarter of the yearly catch. An average of 14 million fish are caught there each winter.

LIFE IN COLD WATER

Surviving the winter in icy water isn't easy. Some fish, such as bass, sunfish, and catfish, slow their breathing and swim around a lot less. They move to the edge of a stream or pond and settle their bodies into mud or leaves. Some fish can even go all winter without eating.

Other fish, such as trout, salmon, and pike, still swim around under the ice. You can find them in the deepest parts of lakes or rivers. This is because the water is warmer there.

HUNTING HINT

Most walleye weigh only about 2 pounds (0.91 kg). However, these fish can grow up to 25 pounds (11.34 kg). That's a prize catch!

Yellow perch stay active during the winter. There's a good chance you'll **catch one** while ice fishing.

BEFORE YOU FISH

Before you go ice fishing, you'll need a fishing license. This is an official paper that says you're allowed to catch fish. Each state has its own rules. Visit your state's wildlife department website for more information.

Check the weather before planning a fishing trip. You wouldn't want your first time out on the ice to be ruined if it's very cold or snowing heavily. Knowing the weather will help you plan what to wear and bring so your first ice-fishing trip will be enjoyable.

An adult who enjoys ice fishing can give you lots of great tips. Remember to never go out on the ice alone.

HUNTING HINT

You'll need to bring a lot of gear when you go ice fishing. A sled can help you carry everything across the ice.

KEEPING WARM

The key to staying warm while ice fishing is layering. This is when you wear one piece of clothing over another. You can remove a layer if you get too hot. A good pair of boots will keep you from slipping on the ice.

You'll also need mittens or gloves, a scarf, and a warm hat. A jacket with **reflective** stripes helps other people see you if it gets dark. Waterproof and windproof gear will help keep you warm and dry while fishing.

HUNTING HINT

Some people use ice skates to get around on a frozen lake. Wearing snowshoes makes it easier to walk when the ice is covered in snow.

Even though it will be cold when you go ice fishing, it could still be sunny. Take a pair of sunglasses to help you see. It's also a good idea to wear sunscreen so your face doesn't get sunburned.

ON THIN ICE

The first and most important thing you should do before ice fishing is check the ice. Thin ice is very **dangerous**. You have to make sure the ice is at least 4 inches (10.2 cm) thick to walk on it and fish safely.

If you fell through the ice, the water underneath would be too cold for your body to stand for long. Ice must be at least 8 inches (20.3 cm) thick before someone can safely drive a snowmobile or car onto it.

HUNTING HINT

Sometimes even thick ice will make strange cracking noises while you're ice fishing. It's usually harmless. If you're worried, check the ice again.

A snowmobile is a faster way to move your fishing gear across the ice. Just be sure the ice is thick enough before driving onto it.

DRILLING A HOLE

You'll need to make a hole in the ice where you want to fish. A special drill called an ice auger is the perfect tool for the job. The hole should not be more than 1 foot (30.5 cm) across.

When ice is not as thick, you can make a hole with an ice **chisel**. A chisel on the end of a pole is used to chop into the ice. If you use an ice chisel, tie it to your arm using string so it won't sink if you drop it.

HUNTING HINT

Some ice augers are turned by hand and some have motors. Only use an ice auger if an adult is nearby to help you.

This man is drilling a hole with an ice auger. Don't let go when the auger breaks through the ice!

REEL IT IN!

There are three different ice-fishing methods to choose from. One way to fish is with a rod and reel. A reel holds your fishing line. The rods used in ice fishing are much shorter than those used in warm-weather fishing. They're usually between 2 and 5 feet (61 and 152 cm) long.

If you catch a fish, you can keep it or release it back into the wild. Check your state's laws before fishing. Your fish may need to be over a certain length if you want to keep it.

HUNTING HINT

Most states have a bag limit. A bag limit is the number of fish you can bring home each day.

More people can enjoy ice fishing if you use the catch-and-release method. Remember to hold the fish gently as you return it to the water.

You can also ice fish using tip-up flags. These are little flags that connect to your fishing line. You set up your line in the water with the flag pointing down toward the surface of the ice. The flag will flip up when a fish bites.

You can also ice fish with a spear. Ice-fishing spears are long poles with several sharp points on the end. You must pay close attention to your fishing hole when spear fishing. When a fish swims into view, jab it with your spear.

HUNTING HINT

You can make several holes in the ice when using tip-ups. You can set up a few flags in a row and keep an eye on all of them.

This Inuit man is using a spear to fish in Nunavut, Canada. The native peoples of the Arctic have a long history of ice fishing.

SAFETY FIRST

Never go ice fishing alone. Always make sure an adult is with you. If you bring a cell phone, keep it dry in a plastic bag. It's also important to bring the right safety gear. Have a **life preserver** nearby in case you or someone you're with falls in the water. You can blow a whistle to get the attention of other people if you need help. It's easy to get lost on a large, snow-covered lake. Bring a **compass** to help you find your way.

HUNTING HINT

If you fall through the ice, get out of the water as fast as possible. Be sure to dry off and warm up quickly once you're out of the water.

Ice fishing is safer with other people. This group is fishing on a frozen river in Russia.

SHELTER FROM THE COLD

If you don't mind the cold, you can sit outside on the ice while fishing. Some people sit on a stool or a bucket. If you don't want to be outside, you can use a shelter. A shelter is a covering that protects you from the wind, snow, and cold.

There are several different kinds of shelters. Windbreaks are shelters that block out the wind on two or three sides. Collapsible shelters fold up. They don't weigh much and are easy to carry around.

HUNTING HINT

Sometimes there are so many ice-fishing shelters set up in an area that it looks like there is a village on the ice!

You don't have to go ice fishing during the day. It gets colder at night, though, so using a shelter is a good idea.

Some ice fishers use shelters that are easily moved around. These are called mobile, or moveable, shelters. These shelters usually have a hard floor and a cloth covering over a metal frame. People usually set them up and take them down each time they fish.

Permanent shelters look like tiny houses. They're usually made out of wood or another sturdy **material**. These shelters can be left on the ice for the entire winter. They're also called sheds, shacks, or cabins.

HUNTING HINT

You can keep snacks and drinks in your fishing shelter. Books, games, a radio, or a small TV will help you pass the time while waiting for a fish to bite.

These permanent **shelters have** small stoves inside to **help** fisherman stay **warm.**

ICE-FISHING FUN

There are many reasons people enjoy ice fishing. Some people fish in large groups. This is a good way to spend time with friends and family. Adults sometimes fish alone and enjoy that quiet time.

There are also people who like taking part in ice-fishing **competitions**. There are usually a number of holes drilled in the ice before a competition begins. Ice fishers have a set amount of time to catch as many fish as they can.

HUNTING HINT

One of the largest ice-fishing events in the world happens each year on Gull Lake in Minnesota. More than 15,000 anglers, or fishermen, fish at more than 20,000 holes drilled into the ice.

Ice fishing is fun for the whole family. Even young children can fish with an adult's help.

FINDING FISH

Some people use special tools to help them find fish under the ice. Underwater cameras are one of these tools. These cameras give fishermen clear pictures of what's under the ice.

Sonar is another useful tool. A sonar device gives off sound waves and picks them up again after they **bounce** off things underwater. Sonar is used to figure out how deep the water is. It's also used to see where weeds and fish are beneath the ice. Ice-fishing **technology** is advancing all the time.

HUNTING HINT

You can watch the images picked up by an underwater camera on a TV in your shelter.

This fisherman is using sonar to locate fish swimming beneath the ice.

29

RESPECTING NATURE

Going ice fishing is a great chance to enjoy the natural world. Be aware of other people fishing around you. Don't be too noisy during your fishing trip. Always clean up any trash before you leave the ice.

Check to be sure you haven't left any fishing line or a baited hook on the ice. Wildlife could be harmed by these objects. Good ice fishers have respect for nature.

HUNTING HINT

Have someone take a picture of you with your first big catch!

GLOSSARY

bounce: To spring back or up after striking a surface.

chisel: A sharp, metal tool used to cut and shape wood, stone, or ice.

compass: A tool for finding directions by using a magnetic needle.

competition: A game or test.

dangerous: Not safe.

life preserver: A device, such as a vest or ring, designed to save a person from drowning by helping them float while in the water.

material: Something from which something else can be made.

permanent: Lasting for a very long time or forever.

reflective: Able to throw back light, heat, or sound.

release: To let go.

technology: A method that uses science to solve problems and the tools used to solve those problems.

INDEX

WEBSITES

Due to the changing nature of Internet links, PowerKids Press has developed
an online list of websites related to the subject of this book. This site is updated
regularly. Please use this link to access the list: www.powerkidslinks.com/hunt/ice